THE GHOSTLY TALES OF OLD TOWN SPRING

Published by Arcadia Children's Books
A Division of Arcadia Publishing, Inc.
Charleston, SC
www.arcadiapublishing.com

Copyright © 2024 by Arcadia Children's Books
All rights reserved

Spooky America is a trademark of Arcadia Publishing, Inc.

First published 2024
Manufactured in the United States

Designed by Jessica Nevins
Images used courtesy of Shutterstock.com; p. 10 AggiePV/File:Wunche Bros. Saloon.JPG/Wikimedia Commons/CC BY-SA 3.0; pp. 2, 82 Nina Alizada/Shutterstock.com.

ISBN 978-1-4671-9763-2
Library of Congress Control Number: 2024939041

Notice: The information in this book is true and complete to the best of our knowledge. It is offered without guarantee on the part of the author or Arcadia Publishing. The author and Arcadia Publishing disclaim all liability in connection with the use of this book.

All rights reserved. No part of this book may be reproduced or transmitted in any form whatsoever without prior written permission from the publisher except in the case of brief quotations embodied in critical articles and reviews.

Spooky America

THE GHOSTLY TALES OF OLD TOWN SPRING

LISHA CAUTHEN

Adapted from Haunted Old Town Spring by Cathy Nance

arcadia
CHILDREN'S BOOKS

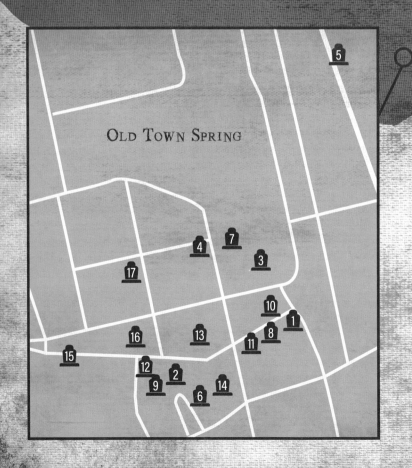

Table of Contents & Map Key

Welcome to Spooky Old Town Spring!...............3

1 Chapter 1. Uncle Charlie and the Wunsche Family Spirits 11

Chapter 2. Working on the Railroad 21
- **2** Lynn's Table
- **3** Puffabelly's Restaurant

Chapter 3. Working at the Mills........................ 31
- **4** Noble Street Tattoo Parlour
- **5** Bayer Lumber Yard

Chapter 4. Life and Death in Old Town Spring 41
- **6** The Dug Out
- **7** Masonic Lodge
- **8** Mallott's Hardware & Variety

Chapter 5. Helpful and Unhelpful Ghosts................... 55
- **9** Chakra Shop
- **10** The Spotted Pony
- **11** Celtic Odyssey Emporium and Spa

Chapter 6. Unearthly Children 69
- **12** Gentry Square
- **13** Little Dutch Girl
- **14** The Indigo Hair Studio

15 Chapter 7. Eerie Dolls, a Haunted Clock, and Earl the Bowling Ball...83

Chapter 8. More than Ghosts 97
- **16** Brookwood Community - Old Town Spring
- **17** The Social Knitwork

A Ghostly Goodbye 105

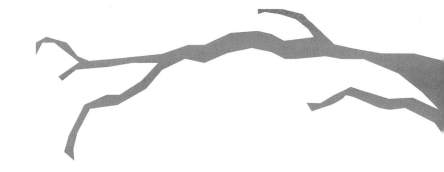

Welcome to Spooky Old Town Spring!

You pick your way carefully around broken glass and splintered wood. You can't believe what you're seeing—the opera house is wrecked, roofs have been blown off businesses and homes, and the railroad roundhouse, switchyard, and depot are utterly destroyed.

It is 1915 in Spring, Texas, and you have just survived a deadly hurricane.

As the story goes, railroad workers named the railroad boomtown north of Houston. They laid the original track across this part of Texas during a terribly hard winter, and by the time the track-laying got to this area, it was spring. The railroad workers were so happy, they dubbed the town "Camp Spring," and later, the name was shortened to "Spring."

The Akokisa (also known as the Orcoquiza) Native people were the first to live here, but they are long gone now. People say the tribe cursed the land so that every time someone cuts down a tree or raises a building in Spring, a fire will break out. But you know better—all the buildings in town are built out of wood and heated with fireplaces and wood stoves, which is a more practical explanation for the frequent fires that plague the town.

You learned in school that the Spaniards were the first Europeans to visit the area in the mid-1700s, and by the 1820s, the first settlers arrived. Most settlers came from Germany, and in the 1840s, after Texas became part of the United States, the government offered land at cheap prices to encourage homesteading. Land near Spring sold for ten to twenty-five cents per acre, and many farmers moved to the area to grow cotton, sugar cane, and vegetables.

Once the Civil War was over, the railroads expanded rapidly into South Texas. The International–Great Northern Railroad Company made Spring a hub for railroad workers. Two different railroads intersect here, and up until the hurricane, Spring has been a boomtown.

The railroads have drawn more businesses and industry to the town, including lumber yards and sawmills, a sugar mill, and cotton gins, where immigrants like your family have found jobs. Hotels, boarding houses, saloons, and a gambling hall serve the rail and mill workers. Families have built houses in Spring, and a bank, hospital, school, churches, post office, and various stores have followed.

You rushed home from school yesterday under darkening skies to see people nailing boards across the windows of their homes. Thankfully, Spring had some warning that the hurricane was coming, so your family could prepare. But it has been so much worse than you thought it would be.

You and your family spent hours on the second floor, clinging to each other as you listened to the wind shriek through the rafters. It rattled the walls and tore at the roof. You watched in horror as the windows bowed under the power of the storm, and you prayed they wouldn't break. Your mother clutched you as water flooded through the first floor. Finally, the wind dropped. The water receded, leaving sludge and debris. Your family's furniture and Mama's Persian rug were a muddy mess.

Now, you and your neighbors are on the street, dazed at the devastation. Grateful to be alive. And you wonder—how will Spring recover?

The truth is, Spring will fall on hard times for a while. The 1915 hurricane severely damaged the rail facilities. This catastrophe will mark the beginning of hard times in Spring, Texas. In 1923, the railroad will decide to move the switching station south to Houston, which is growing faster and bigger than Spring and is closer to the port of Galveston. Railroad workers will leave to follow the work. More people will leave when Prohibition becomes law in 1919. (Prohibition was a law banning the sale and drinking of alcohol.) The saloons will close. Finally, the Great Depression of the 1930s will cause more businesses to shutter and the population of the town of Spring to shrink even more.

But things will get better. A few new businesses will open in the 1960s. The oil boom of the 1970s will fuel further growth, and in the 1980s, local leaders will form the Old Town Spring Association to support popular tourist spots like shops and restaurants. And the Goodyear company will build a gigantic hangar to house its blimp, *America*, nearby.

Old Town Spring started out as a boomtown and has endured disastrous weather, hard economic times, and many tragedies. The result? It has been named one of the most haunted towns in Texas.

Leave the 1915 Hurricane disaster behind and come back to the present to visit today's

Old Town Spring. Go on a ghost hunt to explore the haunted streets and mysterious buildings. Though many people moved away from Spring over the years, some of them came back. And some never left . . .

Wunsche Bros Café & Saloon

Uncle Charlie and the Wunsche Family Spirits

The best place to start your ghost hunt is the oldest commercial structure in Old Town Spring: the Wunsche Bros Café & Saloon. It has stood on its original site at Midway Street and Hardy Road since 1902. The Wunsche brothers, Dell and Willie, immigrated from Germany in 1846. They bought land and farmed, and as Old Town Spring grew, so did the Wunsche family businesses. The family founded a cotton gin, a grist mill, a lumber mill, and Wunsche Bros, a café, saloon, and hotel where railroad workers ate, drank, and rested for the night. The building was also the community's meeting place and one of the few structures to survive the 1915 hurricane that devastated the town.

When you stop by for lunch at the café, look around carefully. You might see shadows or hear unearthly murmurs from hotel guests who have passed on but refuse to leave, but if you're lucky, you might run into the spirit of another member of the Wunsche family: Uncle Charlie.

Locals know that Uncle Charlie Wunsche fell in love with a girl who didn't love him back. Heartbroken, he spent many hours in his room upstairs, pining for his lost love. But he also was a gracious host to the many people who visited his hotel, café, and saloon. He made sure the rooms were clean as a whistle.

He made sure the food was tasty and piping hot. And he made sure his customers had fun. Patrons still hear Uncle Charlie's footsteps as he makes the rounds of the business, pacing from room to room and up and down the stairs, making sure that everything is in order. If it's not, Uncle Charlie will lock doors, knock over tables and chairs, or hide items from the staff.

But when the ghost of Uncle Charlie Wunsche feels sad, you may hear the creak of his rocking chair in his room overhead as he rocks for hours, mourning the girl who didn't love him. You may also see him staring out his upstairs window or sitting on the second-floor porch, watching and hoping his love will return.

One waitress had a very strange encounter with Uncle Charlie. One day, she was carrying a pot of hot coffee in the upstairs hallway. As she passed a room that should have been empty, she saw an older gentleman sitting alone at a table. The man was dressed in a dark suit and wore a hat, which was a bit unusual. The waitress thought the man looked troubled, so she walked up to his table and asked, "Would you like a cup of hot coffee?"

The man abruptly vanished into thin air!

The waitress shivered in the chilled breeze that suddenly swept around her—she had just met heartbroken Charlie Wunsche face-to-face!

Another woman had an eerie encounter in the ladies' bathroom. She was alone in her stall when she suddenly heard the stall door next to her open and slam shut.

The woman jumped. She knew she had been entirely alone in the bathroom. No one had come into the room before her or after her. The woman finished and quickly washed her hands while the tiny hairs on the back of her neck stood up. She felt the hot breath of someone standing behind her, though when she looked in the mirror, she was startled to see she was the only one there.

When the woman got back to her table, she was shaking. She told the waiter about what had happened to her, and he said, "Oh, you met the Wunsche ghost, Uncle Charlie; don't worry, the ghosts are harmless."

If that happened to you, would you believe the ghost was harmless? No one has claimed to have been injured by Charlie Wunsche—just a bit unnerved. Maybe Uncle Charlie was simply making his rounds, checking to make sure the bathroom was spotless.

Poor Uncle Charlie died in 1935 in his room upstairs at the Wunsche Bros Café & Saloon. About a year after he died, an artist moved to town and rented the room. One night, the artist had a weird dream. He dreamed about a man with long white hair wearing a black hat and a black suit. The man was leaning over a table, distraught, when he suddenly jumped up and began to pace.

The artist woke up with a start. The dream bothered him so much he sketched the man, and the next morning, he showed the drawing to some local people. They were stunned—the artist had drawn an exact likeness of Charlie Wunsche. It seems Uncle Charlie's ghost had visited the artist in his dreams.

If you want a chance to snap some pictures of some other Wunsche family ghosts, cross Interstate 45 and visit the Wunsche Family Cemetery, where researchers have caught wispy images of spirits in photographs.

Olena Wunsche is one of the family members buried in the cemetery. In 1929,

Olena and her boyfriend, Edward Stone, were murdered in cold blood. They were found shot to death along the highway—no one knows why, and the murderer was never caught. But some suspect her image has been captured in a photograph. The photo, taken among the headstones at the cemetery, shows the faint image of a woman with prominent cheekbones that might be Olena.

Other photos taken in the cemetery record a man with a white mustache and a gentleman sitting atop a headstone. Are these members of the Wunsche clan, still looking out for Old Town Spring?

It's also believed that the Wunsche family spirits don't stay in the cemetery—they go wandering. One particular phantom often visited a man who lived blocks away. The man was sometimes surprised to find the wayward ghost sitting at his kitchen table drinking a steaming cup of coffee. Why did the ghost visit this man? The man was a descendent of the Wunsche family. Perhaps one of his ancestors just felt like checking in.

The I-45 Diner is in a newer building, but it stands on the old Wunsche family homestead, just across the highway from the Wunsche Family Cemetery. And if you visit the diner at night, you might encounter some of the same things the diner's employees experience all the time. Like hearing their names called when no one is there. Imagine—someone calls your name ... you turn to answer ... and find yourself all alone.

Or are you?

For the best chance of experiencing ghostly activity, visit the diner after dark. That's when you might get poked in the back by unearthly hands, or feel someone invisible brush up against you. Maybe you'll spot the sinister shadow that sometimes hides behind the ice machine.

One night, two workers were closing up the restaurant and getting ready to go home. They turned out all the lights, and as they stood near the front door, an eerie glow suddenly appeared between them. It wasn't coming from the kitchen. It wasn't coming from a streetlamp. It wasn't coming from car headlights in the parking lot. The employees felt goosebumps rise on their arms, and they fled.

Some think the workers were spooked by long-gone Wunsche family members taking an evening stroll. But that's the way it is in Old Town Spring—you never know who you're going to run into. And if you run into a couple of ghosts taking a late-night walk, will you be brave enough to join them?

Working on the Railroad

Thousands of employees of the International–Great Northern Railroad Company passed through Old Town Spring, so it's no surprise that quite a few of their spirits still haunt the streets, buildings, and railroad tracks.

Uncle Charlie isn't the only ghost haunting the Wunsche Bros Café & Saloon. You may also stumble across some long-passed railroad workers who gambled, drank, got into trouble, and occasionally, slept in the building. Visit the upstairs hallway, where many visitors report seeing strange shadows lurking. Unseen entities have been known to visit the women's bathroom. If you stay long enough, don't be surprised if you feel a cold, unnerving touch that lets you know you aren't alone.

Paranormal investigators are certain that many specters still haunt the building because photos have been snapped of apparitions standing on the upstairs porch and looking through the windows. Investigators have also captured disembodied voices during ghost box sessions. A ghost box is a modified radio that continually scans the airwaves, pausing on each frequency for only a fraction of a second. Frank Sumption invented the ghost box, also known as a Frank's box, based on instructions he claimed to have received from the spirit world. Often, researchers will hear one voice that speaks in long phrases or complete sentences, even though the voice has to come from many separate radio frequencies.

One old home where the rail workers refuse to leave is the Bayer house on Aldine Westfield Road. Before lumber baron Gus Bayer owned the building, it was a hotel where rail workers used to stay. Some of the rooms on the second floor still have hotel room numbers hanging above the door. Railroad workers are a hard-working bunch; people still hear them trudging down the stairs and out the door at 4:00 a.m. to report for duty at the old switching station.

You might continue your ghost hunt at the old Doering home, once owned by Henry C. Doering and his wife, Ella Klein. Visitors report seeing the shadow of a man peering out the upstairs window. When Henry died from pneumonia in 1940, Ella had to take in boarders to support their children. Does the ghost of a rail worker still wait in his rented room for a home-cooked supper?

Lynn's Table, formerly Ellen's Café, serves coffee to an otherworldly visitor named Henry, also believed to be a former railroad employee. Henry can be a little tricky—restaurant workers often see him out of the corner of their eye, but when they turn to speak to him, he's gone. Other times, people are astonished to see him as a full-figure apparition walking down the stairs and around the café.

One night, the owner was working alone in her kitchen, when suddenly, she felt something grab her right under the knee. What would you do if you felt a phantom hand squeeze your knee? You might do what the owner did—squeal in fright and run right out of there!

The employees started to leave a cup of

coffee out for Henry with a note telling him they were too busy for games and to please let them get their work done. It seemed to work, but then a strange thing happened.

The café had three letters hanging on the wall that spelled "EAT." Eerily, when the owners opened up one the morning, they found the letters rearranged as "TEA." It began to happen so often, the owner finally bolted the letters to the wall.

And they started serving Henry tea in the morning instead of coffee.

Puffabelly's is a restaurant named for the steam locomotives that pulled trains until the 1950s, when the industry switched to diesel fuel. Puffabelly was a nickname for the early steam engines because they puffed out steam and smoke. You may know the term from the old song, "Down by the Station":

> Down by the station, early in the morning,
> See the little pufferbellies all in a row.
> See the station master turn the little handle.
> Puff, puff, toot, toot!
> Off we go!

If you are brave enough, come to Old Town Spring at night and stake out the railroad tracks near Puffabelly's restaurant. Sometimes, the train-crossing lights flash, but no train ever shows up—at least, no train that anyone can see. Other reports involve mysterious lights on the track that make witnesses think a train is coming, but when they stop their car, no train ever passes. Some have seen sparks, like the sparks from the steel wheels of a train engine running on the track, and others have seen hazy figures.

Probably the most famous railroad

ghost in Old Town Spring is connected to Puffabelly's restaurant. Originally, Puffabelly's operated out of the old Lovelady Depot, a train depot moved from Lovelady, Texas, to Old Town Spring. The Lovelady Depot was built at the same time as the Spring Depot that was lost in the 1915 hurricane, and it looked very similar. With the move, Old Town Spring gained not only a historic building, but also a rather unusual ghost.

It seems that shortly after the depot was constructed in Lovelady in 1902, a train was seen barreling down the wrong tracks. A brave switchman ran toward the oncoming train, frantically waving his lantern to try to stop it. He tripped and fell, and the train ran over him, cutting off his head. His friends carried his body into the depot, where his blood soaked into the floor and left a stain.

Soon, the people of Lovelady started to

see the the brave switchman's headless ghost running along the tracks at night, waving his lantern. And when the depot was moved to Old Town Spring, the switchman's ghost moved with it. Many people in Old Town Spring have been frightened to see his headless ghost running along the tracks near Puffabelly's, waving his lantern and trying to stop a terrible train wreck. He doesn't know that the danger hasn't existed for over 120 years.

If you see him, don't bother to report the sighting to the police. They have taken reports about sightings from unnerved witnesses before, and they know there is nothing they can do to put the switchman's ghost to rest.

Unfortunately, the Lovelady Depot burned down in one of the many fires that seem to have cursed Old Town Spring. The only spot in the building that was left untouched by the fire was the place where the switchman's body was laid on the floor so many years ago.

Today, Puffabelly's looks just like the old Lovelady Depot. The owners scoured the area for used building materials as old as the original depot. Maybe that's why the headless switchman is still there—he feels right at home.

CHAPTER 3

Working at the Mills

Old Town Spring was home to all kinds of different industries in its heyday. The Wunsche family ran a gristmill to grind grain. The Bayer family owned a mill that made packing material out of wood shavings from their sawmill—one of many in town. But perhaps the most popular local mill was the sugar mill.

Cane syrup was a staple in the South. Most families grew their own patch of sugar cane, which they turned into a thick, sweet syrup they could pour on biscuits and corn cakes. In Old Town Spring, the families didn't have to boil their own syrup—they could bring their cane to the sugar mill to have this done.

At the mill, the sugar cane was stripped and then squeezed in a press powered by horses or mules that walked around and around in circles. Then, the cane juice was boiled in giant cast-iron kettles for hours and hours until it turned into a golden syrup. When you pass the field near the historical museum where the sugar mill stood, stay alert. Locals report seeing the misty forms of people carrying their sugar cane to the mill, happy they will soon enjoy syrup drizzled over their morning corn mush.

It was hot work boiling cane syrup at the sugar mill, but work was risky at the lumber mill. Workers were in constant danger of being crushed under toppling stacks of lumber, losing fingers or hands using industrial-sized saws, or being trapped in an accidental fire. But America had to rebuild after the Civil War, and everyone needed lumber. Several lumber yards operated out of Old Town Spring, and it seems some of the workers are still hanging around town.

One place you might see a ghostly worker is the Noble Street Tattoo Parlour. Originally a home, the building was erected in Old Town Spring in 1906 and became a boarding house for lumber mill employees during the last century. Things were quiet in the house until the newest owner started renovating the building in 2017.

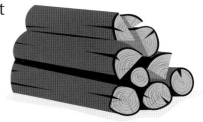

Ghosts don't seem to like change. Hauntings often start when structures are updated or furniture is moved around. While the owner of the Nobel Street Tattoo Parlour was remodeling, everything seemed fine. Then came the grand opening party—and the trouble began.

Everyone was celebrating the opening of the new business, eating and drinking and having a good time. Suddenly, there was a problem—the bathroom door was locked, and no one could open it. That might not seem like a big deal , but after the partygoers pushed and pulled, they realized the door was locked from the inside. Someone had to be in there! Were they sick? Were they hurt? The owner banged on the door, calling, "Are you okay?"

No answer.

Finally, worried that someone needed help

badly, the owner kicked the door in—*bam!* The door swung wildly on its hinges, and the owner exploded into the room to find—

—no one.

Shivers ran up his spine. The lock on the door operated by latch. The latch had to be lifted—there was no way it could fall into place by itself. So how did it happen? Who locked the door? Was it the spirit of a lumber mill worker, angry about all the changes to the building and tired of the loud party? Was the ghost just looking for a little peace and quiet?

If you want another chance to meet a phantom lumber mill worker, visit the Bayer lumber yard on Aldine Westfield Road, where some of the old equipment still sits. The lumber yard has had its share of weird fires over the years.

Some say they were caused by an ancient curse on the land, though others point out that machinery that created sparks and heat and men who smoked cigars and pipes were more likely the causes.

The work was hard and dangerous, so it's safe to say that accidents occurred over the years. But some workers are so fond of the lumber yard, they're still here.

If you ghost hunt at night, keep a sharp eye out. Some have seen strange things on the road that passes by the lumber yard.

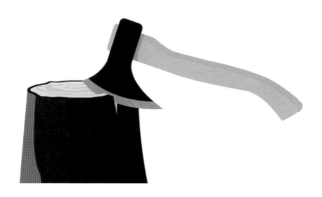

Are they lumberjacks, hauling timber to the yard? Are they sawmill workers, cutting trees into boards? Maybe you'll see happy spirits, like wives bringing baskets of lunch to their husbands. Or the ghosts of frantic laborers carrying a friend to the hospital after a terrible accident.

If you have time to walk around the area, open your phone's voice memo app and hit "record." The lumber yard is a good spot to capture an EVP. EVP stands for electronic voice phenomena, which means voice or sound caught on a tape recorder that no one heard at the time of the recording. You won't hear an EVP while you are recording, you will only hear it when you play back the recording. Researchers believe that spirits can somehow communicate by imprinting these sounds electronically or magnetically on tape or SD cards. Often, researchers will record interviews with clients, and when they play them back later, they hear odd, distinct voices not belonging to anyone present during the meeting.

Anyone they could *see*, that is.

At the lumber yard, ghost hunters have caught EVP that includes the sound of a whistle—like the whistle blown at the sawmill to signal the end of the workday. Maybe you will capture the cheerful tune a phantom worker

sings as he makes his way home at the end of the day. Or maybe you'll catch the desperate cries of someone who needs help. Will you be brave enough to come to the rescue?

Life and Death in Old Town Spring

Many people have lived and died in Old Town Spring. Some died peacefully in their beds. Some died in tragic accidents. Some became ill and wasted away. But even though they passed away many years ago, some residents have chosen to stay.

You'll find one of these ghosts at The Dugout in Doering Court. The Dugout operates out of the old Doering barn, where a terrible accident took place. In the 1930s, Marilyn Doering was playing hide-and-seek with her twelve-year-old friend, Sarah. We aren't sure whether Sarah was hiding or seeking, but somehow, she fell out of the barn's hayloft and broke her leg. Antibiotics were new during the 1930s and not as effective as the prescriptions we have today. Poor Sarah contracted an infection that spread throughout her body, and she died.

Now, witnesses report feeling a rush of cold air while they hear laughing and tiny feet running on the roof. They often hear the joyful sounds of children playing—some people even hear the name "Sarah" called out in the building. Unusual lights can be seen in the barn's loft, and objects are playfully moved around by unseen hands.

Randy Woods, a former assistant press secretary to President Gerald Ford, once worked in the old barn. He believed Sarah and her playmates would watch him work late at night. He often felt creepy cold spots, and when he opened his office in the morning, things would be mysteriously rearranged on his desk. He said in an interview, "I'm a newspaper guy. I'm accustomed to dealing with facts. You've got to experience something like this before you finally say to yourself something unusual is occurring that can't be explained."

Investigators have captured the sounds of a bouncing ball and children giggling on their audio recorders. It seems Sarah and her friends are still playing an eternal game of hide-and-seek.

Will you try to join them? Hiding from ghosts is easy, but do you have the nerve to seek them, too?

If you're looking for even weirder phenomena, take a walk near the Spring Masonic Lodge on Preston Avenue. If you go around to the right side of the building and look at the second window from the back, you may be lucky enough to see the pale ghost of a past lodge member looking back at you.

Then, stand on the gravel road—do you feel rain sprinkles? You might be confused because you won't see any clouds. That's because you're not feeling rain but rather the clammy presence of spirits. Researchers believe that ghosts are so cold, the humidity around them condenses, sometimes producing tiny droplets that fall on us. You may also feel like you are walking through spider webs, though you don't see them. Experts believe this is ectoplasm, which is a gooey substance produced by ghosts when they materialize.

One ghost that you do *not* want to run into

appears at the Bayer home. The Bayer home is a landmark in the Old Town Spring area. Behind it, you will see the smaller, gray house where a doctor once lived and, according to stories, killed himself. People who have lived in the Bayer home believe the doctor is still haunting the area.

One night, some cousins were having a slumber party in the Bayer home. They slept all together on the floor in the dining room. In the middle of the night, three of the cousins woke up, all at the same time. They had felt someone—maybe one of their moms or dads—stepping over and between them in the dead of night, but when they opened their eyes, they were horrified to see that no one was there.

What would you do if that happened to you? Would you go back to sleep? Or would you turn on all the lights and keep watch for the rest of the night?

Some weeks later, the youngest, two-year-old cousin sat watching TV when he looked into the dining room. Suddenly, he began to scream. He said there was a monster coming toward him—a ghastly monster missing part of its face. Was it the poor doctor, still reliving the moment of his death?

The Wunderlich house was the scene of a tragedy before it was relocated behind Puffabelly's restaurant. People say that an unhappily married couple once lived in the house. The husband went out drinking one night, and while he was in town, someone told him that his wife had been seeing another man. The husband came home and confronted his wife and shot her dead. Then he turned the gun on himself.

Hauntings often occur when people die tragically, suddenly, and violently. In this house, paranormal investigators have seen a frightening, dark cloud on the second floor that watches them carefully as they discuss the case. They've captured mysterious images with an infrared camera and have recorded an EVP that sounds like whistling.

Near the Wunderlich house, you'll find the old icehouse. The icehouse is a tiny brick building that was used to refrigerate fresh items before they were sent out on the train. People at that time didn't have electric refrigerators, so they kept things cool with large blocks of ice. However, it's also said that human bodies were kept in the icehouse during the 1800s, before embalming was available. (Embalming is a chemical process that preserves a body after death.)

Many claim that the land where the icehouse stands is a dead zone, a place where no human or animal wants to linger. If you dare visit at night, listen. Do you hear any buzzing insects? Any croaking frogs? Any hooting owls?

Or... are you the only living thing around?

Don't go to the Jailhouse Saloon unless you're ready to have things thrown at you. Many report encountering a phantom man who throws coolers, boxes, and other items. People speculate that the spirit is a former inmate, angry at being locked up. He seems to lash out at certain people that he dislikes. Researchers conducted experiments in the old jailhouse that resulted in an almost back-and-forth conversation. They asked questions and received logical, sensible answers.

When researchers experience communication with a spirit, they consider it an intelligent haunting. An intelligent haunting occurs when a spirit wants to get your attention. An intelligent haunting can happen any time of day or night and feels like you are talking to or interacting with a real person.

One that you can't see.

Investigators at the old jailhouse have also photographed a handprint using a FLIR camera. FLIR stands for forward-looking infrared, which describes a camera that records heat to capture things you can't see with your eyes, especially in the dark. Or things you can't see because they're invisible, like ghosts.

If you're hunting ghosts using a regular camera, check out the old Spring State Bank building, now Mallott's. During the tough days of the 1930s, the bank was the scene of several robberies. At least one robbery resulted in a shootout, and if you look carefully, you can still see some of the bullet holes.

You may even be able to visit the original bank vault. When you visit, listen for noises upstairs or watch for an eerie feeling. If you snap photos, you may catch the ghost that several others have captured in photographs. Their photos show a male with a big nose. They are certain they have recorded a bank clerk eternally trying to stop a robbery. One paranormal team even photographed an apparition of a man wearing a hat and suit jacket from the 1930s, the era when the bank was repeatedly robbed.

About a block away, you'll find Whitehall, one of the few original Old Town Spring homes. It was built by the Mintz family in 1895. Whitehall is constructed in the Victorian style and has twenty-five rooms. Over the years, it's been a home, a boarding house, apartments, a church, a school, offices, and a funeral parlor. Today, if you visit at dusk, you may see the colony of bats that live in the attic fly into the night to feed on insects.

The Klein family lived in Whitehall in the 1920s and 1930s. They owned a funeral home in Tomball, Texas, and when the funeral home burned down in one of the many mysterious fires in the area, the family turned the first floor of Whitehall into a funeral parlor. The embalming room where bodies were prepared was in the back of the house.

It seems that some who have passed to the other side are still around. If you want to know whether there are any ghosts about, check the large dove cage behind the house. The birds coo when a spirit is nearby.

The best-known specters at this location are the Courting Ghosts of Whitehall. Local lore says a couple was coming home from a date in 1933 when a terrible accident occurred. They drove off a bridge into a ravine and were killed instantly. Though their bodies were taken to the funeral parlor in Whitehall, some believe their spirits simply never left. Today, they are said to stay in a secret ghost room inside the house. The couple mostly keeps to themselves, but if you visit when the weather is warm and breezy, you may spot their full-body apparitions on the upstairs porch, swinging together on the swing.

As you look around, notice the remnants of an old treehouse nearby. The boys who built the treehouse abandoned it when the Courting Ghosts scared them away by shaking their tree and making unearthly noises.

Another famous ghost couple has a much happier story. Marie Bailey fell in love with Albert Faetzhold, and though her father forbade the relationship, the two married. They loved to listen to music and dance to their favorite songs. They lived in Old Town Spring, devoted to each other, until their deaths in the 1970s.

After their deaths, the Victrola that Marie had brought from her home in St. Louis was donated to the Spring Historical Museum. A Victrola is an early phonograph that played music that was recorded on a disc. The Victrola had to be cranked by hand to work.

Workers at the museum say that sometimes the Victrola mysteriously plays music by itself—without any hand-cranking—especially after the lights in the museum have been turned off at closing time. Often, the Victrola plays Marie's favorite tunes. Come to Old Town Spring during a full moon, and you may be delighted to see the shadows of a young woman wearing a wedding gown, dancing in the moonlight with her beloved husband.

Helpful and Unhelpful Ghosts

Having a ghost around can be scary. Or it can be a nuisance. Or it can be fun! Some ghosts in Old Town Spring are so helpful, they could almost be considered partners with business owners in the area.

One spirit that helped out in Old Town Spring is the former owner of a building on Gentry Street who took great pride in his business when he was alive. When he died and the new owners took over, he still wanted to rearrange things. The new owners reported that a lampshade would simply not stay put on one of their lamps. No matter how often they put the shade on the lamp, they would soon find it removed and laid aside. It seems the past owner disagreed with their decorating choices!

The new owners also had many toys packed away. One Easter, they found their toy stuffed rabbit placed on a tree stump outside. They were confused—until they found out the previous owner had been very particular about setting a rabbit in the front yard every Easter. His spirit had helped out by plucking the rabbit out of storage and putting it out front to celebrate the holiday, just like he did every year he was alive.

Another store on Gentry Street, the Chakra Shop, hosts a female spirit who brings in shoppers. The owner reports the ghostly woman is about thirty-five years old, wears her hair in a bun, and appears in a white dress popular during the early twentieth century. The owner had been aware of the spirit haunting her shop for some time, but the business partnership between the two ladies started one morning when the owner teased the ghost, asking her to please lead tourists to her store.

The ghost did.

Soon, visitors to Old Town Spring began to show up at the store, claiming they had seen a penny on the sidewalk or in the street. Then another. And another. They had followed the trail of pennies to the Chakra Shop, where they felt a strong urge to go in and look around. There, they would find the perfect item to purchase.

The spirit of the woman in the white dress is so attached to the owner, she followed her when she moved the store to a different building. Who is this helpful ghost? The owner says she is sure the woman had been a resident of Old Town Spring because she recognized the spirit in a photograph at the Spring Historical Museum.

If you stumble across a trail of pennies, follow it. You might find the perfect gift you have been searching for.

One especially helpful ghost hangs out at the Spotted Pony. The relationship between the store owner and her spooky partner began with the paperclip game. At the end of the day, the owner would clear her desk of clutter.

When she came back, she would find a single paperclip in the middle of her desk. This happened over and over again, and she knew it was the ghost's way of getting her attention.

Soon, the owner was sure the ghost was hiding her keys. Annoyed, she would tell him, "Charlie, it's 1:00 a.m., and you better find my keys." Then, she'd hear a noise in the shop, and when she investigated, there would be her keys! The store had mannequins, and Charlie's favorite hiding place for the keys was in one of the mannequins' laps.

But Charlie was good at more than finding keys—once, he even helped the owner solve a crime.

The owner and her employees had gone to the Houston Livestock Show and Rodeo to sell merchandise, but all the money she had made and all the credit card receipts she had collected at the rodeo had been stolen. It was a blow to her business.

Later, the owner was running some errands when she suddenly had the urge to return to her shop and look in the storage shed. That's where she found an employee's backpack—though the cash was gone, all the credit card receipts from the rodeo were there.

A few minutes later, she was walking to her car, backpack in hand, when the employee who owned the backpack showed up. If the owner had been only a few moments later, the employee would have retrieved the backpack and the owner would have never known her employee had stolen from her. She was sure her strange urge to look in the storage shed

was all because of Charlie, who made sure she got there just in time.

Other shop owners have to put up with much less helpful ghosts. The Celtic Odyssey has a ghost that is a bit of a nuisance. The employees are forever hunting for items that are not where they are supposed to be. The store spirit's name is Sydney, and locals recommend that you greet her by name when you visit. If you don't, she gets cranky and makes mischief. The people who work there know it's best to keep Sydney happy.

Another unhelpful ghost once hung out at a bakery formerly on Gentry Street. The bakery owner had to make peace with a spook that was a bit of a bully. The former owner described the ghost as a big man in his mid-sixties who didn't seem to realize that he was dead. He was known to shove people who came to the bakery and block the entrance so the owner couldn't enter her own front door.

Finally, the bakery owner had had enough. She told the ghost that if he didn't stop being mean to her and her shoppers, she would call someone in to drive him out. That got his attention! But she knew he still hung around the bakery because people often reported they felt like they were being watched. At least the spirit stopped pushing people around. He even enjoyed the Christmas holiday bustle, and sometimes the owner would hear him humming seasonal tunes.

Many have experienced the annoyance of a poltergeist haunting. Poltergeist is a German word that means "noisy ghost." Poltergeists are destructive. They break things, move things, and make loud noises. They cause things to appear and disappear. The old Bradley Home on

Main Street is now a shop called Simply Texas, and it has had a trouble-making poltergeist for a while.

The owner reports that when his employees open the store in the morning, they are irritated to find that bottles of hot sauce have been thrown to the ground and broken. Inventory is often moved out of place, and the lights switch on and off on their own. The problems got so disturbing the owner called in a paranormal team to investigate.

The team set up cameras that captured paper flying to the floor when nothing was there to disturb it. They also caught audio evidence of the deadbolt on the front door locking and unlocking by itself. The owner can't stop these things from happening, but he is careful not to disturb the poltergeist any further. When you visit, it may be best to steer clear of the hot sauce shelves.

One former business on Noble Street had to put up with a cranky poltergeist who was fond of water. One day, the owner was rinsing a sign in her bathtub using the showerhead. She had the showerhead pointed away from her, but suddenly, it turned and sprayed her square in the face! She tried to shut off the water, but the showerhead just kept spraying her and everything else in the room!

Finally, she managed to turn off the water. Then she hollered, "Thanks a lot, ghost! I don't want to be cleaning up water all day!"

It may have been a mistake to complain to the poltergeist. A short time later, in the kitchen, a gallon jug of water that had been sitting on the top of the refrigerator managed to tip over, lose its cap, and pour water all over the owner's laptop and paperwork on the table. Which proves it's probably best not to shout at spirits.

One of the oldest original buildings in Old Town Spring is on Midway Street. When you pass by, you may see the misty shape of a faithful dog that has long since passed but still keeps watch on the front porch.

The house was in bad repair, so the people who purchased it started renovations. We know that ghosts don't like change. We know that when homes are fixed up, the spirits often let the living know they are unhappy. And that's what happened on Midway Street.

One poor workman found out what happens when you make a ghost unhappy. He was working under the house, trying to level out the building to stop the walls from cracking and the floor from bowing. The man could

have probably used a little help, but instead, he felt a hard *yank*! Phantom hands had grabbed his legs to pull him out from under the house.

Needless to say, that shook up the workman. Feeling invisible hands clamp around my ankles would have convinced me to find another job—how about you?

CHAPTER 6

Unearthly Children

A group of friends plays a never-ending game of hide-and-seek in the Doering barn; a pair of children plays pranks on the living; and an unknown little girl appears on a spectral swing hanging from a tree on Keith Street. These and many other ghostly children haunt Old Town Spring. If you search the streets and buildings carefully, you might find some of them. Maybe they will even invite you to join in their games.

One former store owner claims she had a pair of child ghosts in residence—Ralph and Polly—who sometimes appear in photographs. Ralph and Polly are happy, rambunctious ghosts, still running up and down the stairs in stores on Gentry Street. Visitors claim they also hear conversations when no one is there. Are they hearing Ralph and Polly making plans for mischief?

Also on Gentry Street, a former business experienced a very active haunting. It started one day when one of the store owners decided to take a nap in the office upstairs. While he was asleep, the bed lifted into the air and then

slammed down again—*bam!* The man was stunned! The experience rattled him so much he never went back upstairs again. Then more frightening things happened in the store.

The store had a corner display with toys for sale, but often, the toys were found strewn around the first floor as if they had been played with. The owners asked the employees if they were responsible, but they denied having anything to do with the misplaced toys.

Later, a psychic visited the shop. (A psychic can look beyond the five senses and use a mysterious sixth sense to gather information.) The psychic did not know the business owners or the things that had happened to them, but she did know what was going on in the building. She told the owners she could see a little boy who said he was sorry he hadn't put the toys away after he'd played with them. He said he would put them away next time. Then the psychic saw some other spirit children and told the owners, "Oh, they're laughing right now. They said they are sorry they scared the man in the bed."

The shop owners' jaws fell open—they were shocked! They hadn't told anyone what had happened upstairs. How did this stranger know? Was she *really* talking to ghost children? And if the answer was yes, where had these ghost children come from?

The mystery was cleared up when an older woman visited the store. She said her family had built the building many years before, and that it had once been the D. Kaplan Feed Store and Dry Goods business. The Kaplan family had lived upstairs above the feed store, and two of the children had died of tuberculosis in the building in the 1920s. Then, in the 1980s, the structure was moved to Old Town Spring. Somehow, the children must have become so attached to their family home they'd stuck around, even though it had been moved twenty-five miles north.

By now, the owners could no longer deny what was happening. They heard someone whistling a tune when no one else was in the store. They heard footsteps upstairs and downstairs. Their mannequins' hair was messed up overnight and had to be rearranged every morning. The activity got to be so much, some of the employees refused to work at night.

Even though the spirit children are a handful, they still have someone keeping a

watchful eye on them in the next realm. A neighboring business owner reported that he sometimes saw a candle lit in the haunted store's upstairs window, and often, a farmer wearing a straw hat. Once, he even thought he saw the apparition of the farmer walking around town, but he couldn't catch up to the farmer before he disappeared.

Would you be brave enough to chase after a ghost?

Continue your ghost hunt close by in Gentry Square. A building at Gentry Square was once a boys' home before it was moved to Old Town Spring. Nowadays, the space can be rented for parties. And the owners knew something was going on from the moment they started fixing up the space. The contractors got spooked when things were thrown at them. As time went on, visitors heard the sounds of bouncing balls and door handles jiggling when no one else was around. One sensitive visitor claims she saw a ten-year-old boy standing outside at a light pole, waiting for his mother. Could this be the spirit of one of the orphans who lived at the boys' home?

The Schoolhouse, also on Gentry Street, was built in 1950 and moved to Old Town Spring in the 1980s. And one former teacher may have decided to come along. The spooky form of a woman has been seen and photographed standing on the porch of the old school at night. Bring your phone along and see if you can capture the ghost, because the photos that have been taken of her are startlingly clear.

But the teacher didn't come alone. Some naughty children may have also traveled with the building, because across the street at the Little Dutch Girl shop, chairs in the courtyard are often rearranged, and sometimes, plopped on top of the roof!

Several charming cottages were moved from Houston, Texas, to Preston Avenue in Old Town Spring. Indigo Hair Studio in the blue cottage on Preston Avenue has experienced activity for many years, stemming back to when other businesses occupied the building. Items fly off shelves, and once, a ten-pound object left the shelf, hung in midair, then slammed to the ground!

Formerly, a pet store occupied the space, and the dog cages would be opened by invisible hands every night. Before that, the building housed a bookstore, and the owner was often spooked by melodies from an unseen music box and stacks of books flying across the room. Nearby, a shop sold clocks. Every day, the business owner would set all the clocks to the correct time. But when he came back in the morning, he was annoyed to see every clock set to 10:10.

Who is responsible for all this mischief? One resident thinks he knows, because he has seen and even talked to the ghost of a little girl who says her name is Shelly. He is certain that Shelly is responsible for unlocking the dog cages and throwing things around. Shelly, who appears to be about eight years old, is rumored to be a spirit who lived during the Civil War. Did she live in Old Town Spring? Or did she arrive with the cottages that were moved from Houston?

One local decided she wasn't going to put up with any nonsense from Shelly. She had a one-sided talk with Shelly and said, "Look, we are going to be here for a while. We are going to have a good time, and you're going to love it. We respect you, and we just hope that you respect us and the fact that we have a business to run here."

That owner hasn't had any problems since.

The former Sedona Joe's on Main Street is said to be the old Sellers family home. Many hair-raising things have happened in the building. One artist who works in the building says he's seen many tenants come and go because of the hauntings. Some were so terrified they left in the middle of the night!

The artist's wife had an unnerving encounter. While moving into the space, the wife asked her artist husband, "Who's this little girl?" The artist was confused—he saw no one. And when the wife looked back, the girl was gone.

The building owners keep a basket of toys under a table that the phantom girl is welcome to play with—and they know she does, because they find the toys scattered around. The spirit also likes to fiddle with angel ornaments that hang from the ceiling. Once, she pulled so hard on the spring holding an angel, the spring straightened out and has never recoiled again.

A sadder story about a child spirit involves a Ferris wheel and a traveling carnival that passed through Old Town Spring many years ago. A little boy and his father were riding the Ferris wheel, enjoying being up high where they could see the whole countryside.

Unfortunately, something went wrong, and the little boy fell out of the ride. His injuries were fatal. Today, if you explore behind the shops in the Gentry Street area, you may run into a little boy looking for his father. But if you stop to help, the boy will vanish into thin air. You may also see the ghost of a man believed to be the boy's father, looking for his lost son.

Child hauntings seem very sad. It's not pleasant to think about children being stuck somewhere in time, but this type of phenomenon may not be exactly what it seems.

Researchers say though ghosts may appear to the living as children, they may not have been children when they passed. They may have lived an entire life and died in old age, but they appear as children because it was when they were the happiest.

Child hauntings might also be residual hauntings. A residual haunting is like a recording of an event that plays over and over again, and sometimes, the living see it. In a residual haunting, the spirit is not actually present. It's like watching a ghost's life in a video or movie. So, if you see a ghost that appears at the same time of day or year repeatedly, or performs the same action over and over again without interacting with the living, you're probably watching an incident from the past that was imprinted on the pages of time.

Same time, same place—it's easy to fit a residual haunting into your schedule. But do you have the nerve to keep an appointment with a ghost?

The Doll Hospital in Old Town Spring

Eerie Dolls, a Haunted Clock, and Earl the Bowling Ball

Hauntings happen for many different reasons and in many different ways. Intelligent ghosts may interact with the living. Residual ghosts may reenact a moment from their lives over and over again. Poltergeists may throw things, hide things, or make a racket. But a common type of haunting many of us experience without even knowing it is a place memory.

A place memory is a feeling or memory attached to an object that echoes something that happened in the past. For instance, a backpack at a second-hand store might have once belonged to someone who liked to hike. If any psychics pick up that backpack, they may "see" the former owner tromping through the woods, whistling a happy tune. But you might pick up the backpack and just feel happy, like the original owner did. You might suddenly feel like taking a walk in the woods, or even start to whistle, without knowing why.

Many objects in Old Town Spring carry place memories. A former business owner on Main Street had a haunted rocking chair. The chair had sentimental value to the owner because her friend, Luther, had passed away while sitting in the chair. The rocking chair was not set on runners—it was a platform rocker that worked on a spring. This chair was famous for rocking all by itself, which is not an easy thing for a platform rocker to do. Once, the owner entered the room and saw the rocker lean all the way back and then spring forward rapidly, as if someone had suddenly stood up. She was sure it was Luther, standing to greet her like a gentleman should. If you sat in the chair, do you think you would feel the peace Luther felt rocking in his chair and the love he had for his friend?

For a time, Old Town Spring hosted reenactments of Civil War battles, complete with actors wearing period clothing and firing black powder guns. Through reenactments, participants bring history to life for an audience. They use the same equipment and tools soldiers used during the Civil War and even cook and eat the same food they would have cooked and eaten in the 1860s.

During some of the reenactments, glowing balls were captured on film. Apparitions of Civil War soldiers materialized—one was a horrifying, disfigured man standing right in the middle of Thyme Square. But no Civil War battle ever took place in Old Town Spring. Where did these bizarre beings come from?

Old Town Spring once housed a Civil War museum, and experts speculate that some of the artifacts housed in the museum carried place memories. Perhaps your ancestor's saber or butternut coat was in the museum, with his memories and feelings still attached.

Maybe you can be the first to discover a place memory haunting at the Doll Hospital on Gentry Street. If your doll somehow gets damaged, this is the place to take it. Dolls from as early as the mid-1700s are in residence, well-loved and waiting to find new homes.

A research group conducted a Frank's box investigation on the front porch of the building and communicated with something intelligent. When asked how old the spirit was, it replied, "Five," and "Eight." When asked if any evil dolls were in the hospital, the Frank's box came back with the chilling answer, "You betcha."

However, the owner disputes that. She claims that nothing out of the ordinary has ever happened to her in the Doll Hospital. Maybe the spirit talking through the box wasn't really connected with the Doll Hospital at all. It's much more likely that when you visit and hold one of the dolls, you will feel all the fun the previous owner had playing with and loving the doll. And maybe you can give that doll a new home.

Another doll in Old Town Spring has displayed unexplainable phenomena. At Kudos Gift Shop, an uncanny doll that seems to change expressions sits in the front window. Most of the time, the doll appears normal. But some witnesses have had the creepy experience of seeing her open her mouth slightly. As they watch, little by little, the doll opens her mouth wider and wider, and then finally, it displays a tooth! If you have the nerve, come at night and set your camera phone to "burst." See if you can catch the transformation that others have described.

Several haunted items cause trouble at Cathy Nance Studios on Gentry Street. When the owner first occupied the building, she would make sure the lights were off and the air conditioner was set correctly before she left for the evening. But when she opened up in the morning, she'd find the lights on, the air conditioner set to odd temperatures, and items moved from their places. At first, Cathy thought the landlord was responsible. Then she found out the previous owner had brought African artifacts into the building. Were place memory hauntings from the African artifacts responsible for the weird activity? It's hard to know, because the current owner has also brought haunted items into the building.

Cathy Nance is also a paranormal investigator, and on one of her haunted house cases, she came across a clock. It seems some Oklahoma homeowners had found the old clock in their attic. When they brought it down, polished it up, and wound it, problems began. They claimed unseen spirits physically harmed them. So, they gave the clock to a researcher to see if he could handle it.

The researcher took the clock home, which was a mistake. He set the clock on his bedroom dresser and immediately had eerie things happen to him.

First, he heard someone walking around in the empty hallway outside his bedroom. Then, he heard a weird ticking coming from the clock. Finally, the doorknob on his bedroom door began to shake—and then locked itself! Hands trembling, the researcher searched the home, but it was plain that he was alone.

Later, while the researcher took a bath, the glass door on the front of the clock opened by itself. When the researcher saw this, he decided to wind the clock to see what would happen.

Nothing happened. At first. But in the middle of the night, when the researcher was sound asleep, he was startled awake to see orange spiders all over the room and the clock making a grinding, mechanical noise that sounded like laughter.

The researcher had had enough. He returned the clock to the homeowners—but they didn't want it. They wouldn't even let it into their house. It sat outside on their porch.

That's when Cathy Nance, the studio owner, agreed to take it off everyone's hands. She hasn't had any problems with the clock because she doesn't wind it. If she does, the clock will almost certainly come alive—and then who knows what will happen?

Cathy is also the caretaker of a haunted bowling ball. A woman she met had a bowling ball with the name "Earl" engraved on it. Earl the bowling ball did strange things. Once, the woman was talking to a neighbor in her living room when Earl slowly rolled down the hallway, all by itself. It came to a stop in front of the woman. Puzzled, the woman watched the bowling ball start rolling again and then stop at her neighbor's feet. While the women stared at Earl in shock, it started to roll away.

The neighbor snapped out of her trance, grabbed Earl, and threw it outside.

But things still continued to happen. The lights turned on and off. Things moved around the house. The woman was sure Earl was responsible, so she buried the bowling ball in her yard. Unfortunately, her dog dug it up.

Next, the woman put Earl in a crevice in a large tree so it couldn't move. Still, bad things kept happening in her home.

Cathy offered to take Earl, and the woman eagerly agreed. To this day, Earl the bowling ball sits in Cathy's studio, making trouble. (Luckily, it's the type of trouble she can live with.)

The owner of the Spotted Pony has many interesting stories to tell, including the story of the unknown girl in the photo. At an auction in 1990, the owner acquired the photo of a young girl taken in the 1940s. No one knew who she was or where she came from. The owner took a liking to the unknown girl and hung the photo at her place of business, but her employees said the photo made them so uncomfortable, they would not return to work. So, the owner took the photo home with her and hung it in a closet facing the wall.

Sometime later, she moved her business to a new location and brought the unknown girl's photo to the new store. When she and an employee hung the picture, they were astonished to see the unknown girl in the photo smile. Were they seeing things? No, they agreed that they knew what they had seen—the unknown girl had smiled at them. Maybe she was happy to be out of that closet!

When you visit the Spotted Pony, ask to see the photo of the unknown girl. If you watch her carefully as you walk from one end of the room of the other, you may see her eyes follow you.

While she smiles.

More than Ghosts

Old Town Spring is alive with unexplainable activity, but not all of the phenomena are ghosts. Investigators have discovered areas in town where scientific instruments produce bizarre readings. Others sense the presence of entities that are not, and have never been, human.

One place to look for nonhuman spirits is the former Brookwood Community Store on

Gentry Street. Brookwood is a nonprofit that helps people with disabilities, and its store in Old Town Spring raised funds for the services Brookwood provides.

The store was fully staffed, but there were more helpers in the building than were on the payroll. Security cameras on nearby businesses continually captured mysterious, flickering lights floating around inside the store when it was closed. One neighbor was so concerned that someone had broken into the store, she investigated. After a thorough search, she found no one was there.

But maybe someone really was there—angels. Locals believe the community has a troop of angels watching over it, and some of these angels may even have taken an interest in protecting the community's store!

Paranormal investigators often capture another type of mysterious light in their photographs—orbs. Orbs are balls of light that many believe are wandering spirits. However, photographs of orbs may not be what they seem. Dust and insects may appear as orbs in photographs. Most professional researchers dismiss orbs as evidence of supernatural activity, unless they can see them with their own eyes or they radiate their own light.

The courtyard where you will find the post office and gazebo is a good place to hunt for true orbs. Reports indicate a green orb can often be seen in the area. The green orb seems to be attracted to certain people and will dance around them. Is it an angel, an elf, or the soul of an animal? No one knows. Many people have seen the green orb, and some have been lucky enough to catch it in photographs. Take

as many photos as you can because it will increase your chances of going home with a piece of eerie evidence.

If you're ready for even more eerie experiences, don't miss checking out the gazebo. People often report feeling dizzy or nauseated when they stand or sit in it, or they may feel tingling or vibrations. Some residents think the gazebo is located at an unearthly portal or gate to another world. Others claim the gazebo sits on a vortex, which is a spiraling spiritual energy that you can't see but *can* feel. Ghosts and other spirits are often attracted to vortexes because they can sense them. To a supernatural being, a vortex looks like a candle flame flickering in the dark. Will you sit in the gazebo for a spell and see what you feel?

Another good place to look for ghosts and other spirits is near the well on Main Street. First, many of the cottages around the area have been moved from other towns and are full of their own memories and hauntings. Second, the well is like a supernatural phenomena generator. That's because moving water is believed to create a magnetic field that ghosts and spirits can use to materialize. Investigators have measured the area in Old Town Spring and have recorded occasional spikes in the electromagnetic field (EMF).

Investigators measure EMF frequencies at haunted sites with meters. Abnormally high EMF can be caused by improper electrical wiring, but some also believe high EMF indicates the presence of spirits. EMF has been proven in the laboratory to affect the human body. It can cause sleep disturbances, anxiety, and hallucinations, if it is severe enough.

But then again...so do ghosts and other strange beings.

Over on Keith Street, behind the Social

Knitwork shop, stands a grove of trees. Some believe these are very special trees that speak to each other through their roots. As the story goes, fairies live among these trees, where they are nurtured and protected. Neighbors even report seeing fairies flitting among the leaves. When you investigate, be sure to lay your hands on the trees so you can feel their energy tingle up your arms. If you take some photos, you might capture some interesting evidence of the Old Town Spring fairies.

Strange lights have been seen all over Old Town Spring. Some believe these lights are unidentified flying objects (UFOs). Preservation Park on Spring School Road is said to be the site where many unexplained lights have been seen and videoed. One night, a resident went outside to watch a meteor shower, but he saw much more. He saw many, many white balls of light chasing each other inside a single cloud.

Others have recorded unexplainable lights in the sky all over Old Town Spring. Are these lights coming from aliens visiting the people who live and work in Old Town Spring? Maybe they know they will be greeted warmly. After all, the locals are used to strange happenings!

A Ghostly Goodbye

Old Town Spring is a fun, friendly place. Tourists come to enjoy delicious food, interesting shops, lively music, and fascinating history. But some visitors—like you—know there's more to explore.

Ghosts, a haunted bowling ball, fairies, and UFOs—Old Town Spring has it all. But are they real? Does anyone know for sure? Some think they can prove the existence of ghosts by taking photographs. Some rely on audio recordings. Others chart EMF readings and FLIR readings, and still others trust their gut. In the end, each of us has to make up our own minds based on our research and experiences, and decide—are ghosts and other strange beings real?

What do you believe?

LISHA CAUTHEN grew up near Old Town Spring among the haints and ghost lights of the Texas Gulf Coast. She currently writes in the attic of a 100-year-old house built on a Civil War battlefield in Kansas City, Missouri. Which is only a little bit haunted. This is her fourth book of Ghostly Tales in the *Spooky America* series.

Check out some of the other *Spooky America* titles available now!

Spooky America was adapted from the creeptastic *Haunted America* series for adults. *Haunted America* explores historical haunts in cities and regions across America. Here's more from the original *Haunted Old Town Spring* author, Cathy Nance.